Serenity's Quarantine Life

Serenity Carter

Serenity's Quarantine Life

Serenity's Quarantine Life

Serenity Carter

Contents

Half Title Page 3

Full Title Page 5

Copyright Page 7

Epigraph 9

Contents 11

Acknowledgments- 14

Introduction 1

Day One 1

Day Two 2

Day Three 3

Day Four 4

Day Five 5

Day Six 6

Day Seven 7

Day Eight 8

Day Nine 9

Day Ten 10

Day Eleven 11

Day Twelve 12

Day Thirteen 13

Day Fourteen   14

Day Fifteen   15

Day Sixteen   16

Day Seventeen   17

Day Eighteen   18

Day Nineteen   19

Day Twenty   20

Day Twenty-One   21

Day Twenty-Two   22

Day Twenty-Three   23

Day Twenty-Four   24

Day Twenty-Five   25

Day Twenty-Six   26

Day Twenty-Seven   27

Day Twenty –Eight   28

Day Twenty-Nine   29

Day Thirty   30

About The Author –   31

Acknowledgments-

I want to take time to give a special shoutout to three of the most important people in my life. These people have brought me to where I am right now. I love you Tameka Morris-Cooper, Taymanie Carter and Jennifer Gilbert.

Introduction

My name is Serenity, and this is my events during the quarantine. During this quarantine, I've had to ask my parents a lot of questions. With each answer there grew another questions. So, when you read this book you are going to find out how I survived my quarantine.

Day One

Even though people are getting extremely sick, I really wish we could still be able to go out. But I don't think anyone wants to go outside because it's a possibility that they would and/or could get sick. On a different note just stay away from everybody and don't be around a lot of people. Stay 6ft away.

Day Two

Me and my sisters painted the chairs...just for a little fun. By the time we were done we were hungry. We went to a seafood place and bought us some seafood. When we got back home it was nighttime, so we played cards for a little while. My quarantine life is very boring.

Day Three

Every now and then I would talk with my friends from my old house. I would call my God sister and we would talk on the phone for a little while. Since we have been quarantined, we haven't been able to see each other that much.

Day Four

Today wasn't such a good day. Me and my sisters got into an argument. If case you guys didn't know, I have an unbelievably bad attitude. I really have been trying to work on it and I really think I have been doing good so far. I have been trying so hard to keep my attitude together. But sometimes it just burst out. My mom always try to tell me to ignore them.

Day Five

I really don't like the idea of Covid-19. It really changed my life a lot. My life was incredibly fun before this virus came out. It's kind of boring now that we can't go outside. That's very weird because when we weren't quarantined, we never went outside. But now that we can't go outside, it's like we are very eager to go outside.

Day Six

Today was a chill day! I watched my sister do hair for a little while. I rode with my mama to my aunt's house, and we sat over there for a little while. When we left from over then we went straight home. By the time we got home it was 4:00pm. Our dog had an appointment at 4:30pm so we picked up my sister Imani and we went to her doctor. After we got back from the doctor, we decided that we wanted seafood. We went to get some seafood and it only took about 10 minutes. It was so good! As you can see, me and my family love seafood.

Day Seven

Today my mama ordered us new masks! I'm so excited! A few days later our mask got here "yay"! They are so pretty. Even if we are not going anywhere, I still just wear it around the house. But if I wear it for too long it gets ridiculously hot. Besides that, we love them. We were so happy when we saw the package on the porch.

Day Eight

My mama had to do hair today. When her client got here, she got straight to it. I helped her do hair just because I was very bored. Once we got done doing her hair, we cleaned up our mess. When we got done cleaning up, I went outside and rode my bike for a little while. After I got tired of riding the bike I went in the house and made me something to eat. By the time I got done eating I was tired, so I took a nap.

Day Nine

Quarantine is so boring! I have nothing to do but sit around all day. Me and my family basically just play around making each other laugh. I don't think anybody like the idea of being quarantined. We can't go to parks, we can't do anything! It's just so boring!

Day Ten

When I woke up today, I did not feel good at all! My stomach was hurting so bad. I got out of bed and went downstairs and laid on the couch. Eventually I fell asleep when I woke up, I felt much better. The nap really helped; my stomach didn't hurt for the rest of the day. So, from now on, I know what to do.

Day Eleven

I really like the new house, but I also miss my friends from the old house. The old house was incredibly fun, and we had a lot of fun there. I am kind of mad that we moved, but I'm happy that we moved to something bigger and better.

Day Twelve

It was so boring today! All I did when I woke up was ride the bike, then come back in the house. Every time I would come in the house, I would drink water and sit on the couch. I had nothing else to do! "It's so boring!" Why do we have to be quarantined? There's nothing to do.

Day Thirteen

I really miss my God family so much! It's like before Covid-19, we were with them almost every day. But now we hardly even see them. I miss them like they were my blood family. I really wish we weren't quarantined. I miss them so much.

Day Fourteen

Sometimes I really don't understand. Like this pandemic is just so crazy. It came out of nowhere! It just popped up and got worse and worse! It's just so sad and boring. The world was perfectly fine without this pandemic. I really wish it were over.

Day Fifteen

The thing that I miss most is going outside and being with my God family. If I don't miss anything else that's the two things that I miss. I really wish we could see them and that I could go outside. I can't wait until this is over. I won't stop saying this until this is over. It's so boring.

Day Sixteen

If you didn't know, me and my sister Miracle praise dance. My God mama oversees the group. I really enjoy doing it, and I feel like that is my passion. That is what I want to do. It's an incredibly fun thing to do and I think a lot of people would like to do it. We started off small and we started growing more and more. But since Covid-19 started, we haven't been able to practice.

Day Seventeen

My God family and I have so much fun together. Sometimes we would go to parks for a picnic and play games. But we can't because we're quarantined. "That sucks, yeah I know". We would go to the park to practice sometimes. After we practice, we would play for a little while.

Day Eighteen

As soon as this pandemic is over, the first thing I want to do is go see my God family. I'm going to be so excited. I'm going to spend so much time with them. This pandemic is separating us more and more and I really wish that it would be over. We were getting closer and closer. They are the thing that I miss most. They are on the top of my list of the things that I miss the most.

Day Nineteen

When I don't go outside to ride the bike, I just watch YouTube. When I'm bored and no one can find me, I'm probably somewhere watching YouTube. I watch it all day and I stay missing from everyone the whole day. Since the quarantine, my sisters and I are closer, but sometimes I need my space. I went to eat and back to my room till I fell asleep.

Day Twenty

I was the first one to wake up in my house. I made me some breakfast and sat on the couch to watch YouTube. I didn't know what to watch because I had watched all the videos of the people that were dancing, those doing funny things and crazy stuff and I was still bored. On that note, I went in the backyard to practice since I had nothing else to do. As I was practicing, I was also exercising. My God Mama told me to practice even when I'm not at practice. So that's what I did. I ended my day playing cards with my sisters.

Day Twenty-One

"How do I feel about us being quarantined"? I feel like if we don't stay home it's going to take longer for the government to open our city and our state. The more people that go outside, the longer it will take. I can't wait until my state opens so we can finally go places. But right now, we can't go anywhere. All the stores close early now. There's nothing to do!

Day Twenty-Two

It feels like it has been a million days already! But sadly, it hasn't. I can't wait until this is over! It's so boring because there's nothing to do. All I can do is go on the porch and ride the bike outside. I have never been this bored.

Day Twenty-Three

Today is my aunt's birthday! She is having a little family get together even though were quarantined. Since we were the first to arrive, no one had made it yet. Once inside I began jumping on the trampoline the whole time, it was incredibly fun. They made my favorite… seafood! I was so happy! We were the last to leave the party. But the most important fact is that I had fun.

Day Twenty-Four

I don't think anybody wants to be sick. But for you not to get sick, you will always have to wear your mask, keep your hands washed, and try not to be around anyone that is sick. If you are sick, I would advise you to stay home. Quarantine yourself. This virus is deadly and if you feel like you're getting sick stay home. If you're sick and you are around people you can get them sick.

Day Twenty-Five

A few days ago, my grandmother mom passed away. Since we're quarantined, we couldn't have a funeral. So, my aunt decided to have a balloon release. We released the balloons. We sat down, ate, listened to music and was just vibing. After a little while, we played Uno. The Uno game was so fun. Again, we were the last to leave and that's almost anywhere we go.

Day Twenty-Six

My mom bought a pool to put in the backyard. Today it was very sunny. We blew up the pool and we played in there for a little while. It felt so good it felt like we were in the real pool. We stopped the ice cream truck and bought us some ice cream. Then we got back in the pool for a little while.

Day Twenty-Seven

I asked my mom to take me to the dollar store so that I can get me some candy. When we went in the store, I saw this new Elmer's Glue Slime. I bought the pink one and the clear one. They are so pretty! The clear one is so spotless. I love them! By the way, I didn't forget to get my candy.

Day Twenty -Eight

Have yall ever been so bored to where all you want to do is sleep? Well if so, don't feel bad because that's how I am during this quarantine. I basically sleep all day to the point where sleeping gets boring. Yeah, I know that sucks!

Day Twenty-Nine

Today was a super chill day. We sat in the bed all day watching tv. The only time I went anywhere was to eat and that was downstairs. When my phone died, I watched tv. When I got tired of watching TV, I went to sleep. I was so tired! My eyes felt like they were going to burn off.

Day Thirty

Today is my God brother Taylor's birthday! He was having a little quarantine get together. I arrived at his party with my sisters. I was excited because we really haven't been to see my God brother as much since quarantine! I gave him his birthday present and began enjoying the party. The theme was tie dye, so we all made our shirts and let them sit. We played games outdoors and had a lot of fun. Before too long, we ate, then sang happy birthday. My mom came to pick us up, and I was tired from all the dancing and hanging that happened today. I ended my day after my bath.

About The Author –

Hello my name is Serenity Carter and I was born on October 31, 2007. My favorite color is pink and red. I am a part of a praise dance group. This praise group changed my life a lot! I love it and it's my passion.